THE OUR FATHER

By AGNES AND SALEM DE BEZENAC

with REV. THOMAS J. DONAGHY

Illustrated by AGNES DE BEZENAC

Colored by SABINE RICH

REGINA PRESS
New Jersey

2

Our Father, Who art in heaven,

We are praying to God.
He is our loving Father in heaven.

hallowed be Thy name;

Hallowed means "holy" or "great."
It's like saying, "Your name is awesome!"

Thy kingdom come,

God's kingdom is a loving place to be.

7

8

Thy will be done
on earth as it is in heaven.

God wants us to live in peace and
with goodness, so that the earth
will be like heaven.

Give us this day our daily bread,

We trust that God will give us
what we need each day.

*and forgive us our trespasses,
as we forgive those who
trespass against us;*

We're asking God to forgive us
for our mistakes, and we promise
to forgive people who have
done wrong to us.

14

and lead us not into temptation,
but deliver us from evil.

We're asking **God** to help us to do the right thing, even when that's hard to do.

More
Prayers for You

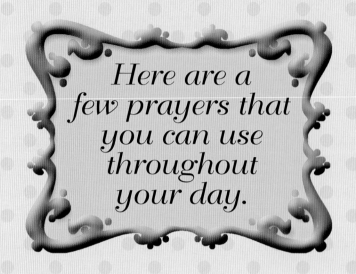

Here are a few prayers that you can use throughout your day.

20

O God, we are always in Your sight,
from light of day to dark of night.
Each day, may we be aware
of Your tender, loving care.

Rev. Thomas J. Donaghy

21

Each day, may our voices raise
a joyful hymn of thankful praise
for every gift we receive anew
from our God Who is ever true.

Rev. Thomas J. Donaghy

We pray to You in heaven above;
it is from there You send Your love.
We know that You want us to share
with all we meet Your gentle care.

Rev. Thomas J. Donaghy

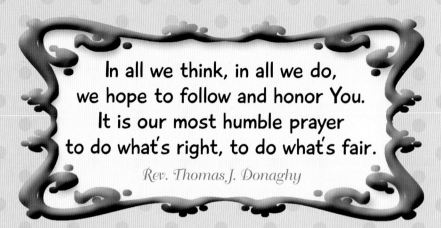

In all we think, in all we do,
we hope to follow and honor You.
It is our most humble prayer
to do what's right, to do what's fair.

Rev. Thomas J. Donaghy

24

Dear God, bless my little friends,
and bless my big friends, too.
Help us to show lots of love
and grow up to be like You.

Agnes de Bezenac

25

Dear God, You make all things good;
You give us warmth, You give us food.
You provide for our every need;
we are most grateful—yes, indeed!

Rev. Thomas J. Donaghy

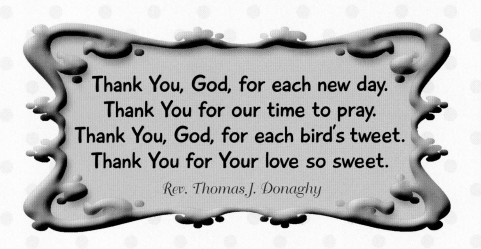

Thank You, God, for each new day.
Thank You for our time to pray.
Thank You, God, for each bird's tweet.
Thank You for Your love so sweet.

Rev. Thomas J. Donaghy

Now that the day is done,
I stop to think about You.
Thank You that You are near
so that I have nothing to fear.

Agnes de Bezenac

Jesus, thanks for being here tonight.
I'm never out of Your sight.
You're like a warm blanket over me.
That's just the way I like it to be.

Salem de Bezenac

All the stars we see tonight,
they reflect Your light so bright.
They will watch us as we sleep,
and our souls, O God, You'll keep.

Rev. Thomas J. Donaghy

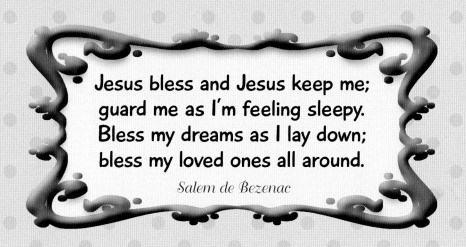

Jesus bless and Jesus keep me;
guard me as I'm feeling sleepy.
Bless my dreams as I lay down;
bless my loved ones all around.

Salem de Bezenac

FIRST BIBLE™ COLLECTION AND BABY BLESSINGS™ BOARD BOOKS

Catholic Baby's First Bible
Edited by Judith Bauer
Illustrations by Colin & Moira MacLean

This board book Bible is beautifully illustrated with peek-through windows and has sold well over 1 million copies. It contains a treasury of Bible stories beginning with Creation and ending with the Resurrection.
RG10410 Size: 6" x 7½". 20 pages.
ISBN 978-0-88271-714-2

Baby Blessings Catholic Bible
Written by Alice Joyce Davidson
Edited by Judith Bauer
Illustrations by M. Stanley & J. Smith

Baby Blessings Catholic Bible gives parents and caregivers a positive and enjoyable way to teach children about the Bible. From Creation through Easter, some of the best-loved stories from the Old Testament and New Testament are presented in delightful rhyme and illustrated in glowing color. There are special prayers and discussion questions, which make it a rich interactive experience for parents and children.
RG15020 Size: 6½" x 7¾". 24 pages.
ISBN 978-0-88271-125-6

Catholic Baby's First Prayers
Edited by Judith Bauer
Illustrations by Peter Stevenson

This board book is beautifully illustrated with peek-through windows and has sold well over 1 million copies. It contains a treasury of prayers including the Guardian Angel Prayer, the Our Father, and the Hail Mary.
RG10411 Size: 6" x 7½". 20 pages.
ISBN 978-0-88271-715-9